RWANDA 2016 HUMAN RIGHTS REPORT

EXECUTIVE SUMMARY

Rwanda is a constitutional republic dominated by a strong presidency. The ruling Rwandan Patriotic Front (RPF) led a governing coalition that included four smaller parties. In 2010 voters elected President Paul Kagame to a second seven-year term with 93 percent of the vote. Three other registered political parties participated in the presidential election. In 2013 elections were conducted for parliament's lower house, the Chamber of Deputies. Candidates from the RPF and two other parties that supported RPF policies won all of the open seats, and election observers reported numerous flaws, including possible irregularities in the vote tabulation process. In 2015 the country held a constitutional referendum; the National Electoral Commission reported 98 percent of registered voters participated, and 98 percent endorsed a set of amendments that included provisions that would allow the president to run for up to three additional terms in office.

Civilian authorities maintained effective control over state security forces (SSF).

The most important human rights problems were government harassment, arrest, and abuse of political opponents, human rights advocates, and individuals perceived to pose a threat to government control and social order; security forces' disregard for the rule of law; and restrictions on media freedom and civil liberties. Due to restrictions on the registration and operation of opposition parties, citizens did not have the ability to change their government through free and fair elections.

Other major human rights problems included arbitrary or unlawful killings; torture and harsh conditions in prisons and detention centers; arbitrary arrest; prolonged pretrial detention; government infringement on citizens' privacy rights and on freedoms of speech, assembly, and association; government restrictions on and harassment of some local and international nongovernmental organizations (NGOs), particularly organizations that monitored and reported on human rights and media freedoms; some reports of trafficking in persons; and government restrictions on labor rights; and child labor.

The government in many cases took steps to prosecute or punish officials who committed abuses, including within the security services, but impunity involving civilian officials and the SSF was a problem.

Section 1. Respect for the Integrity of the Person, Including Freedom from:

a. Arbitrary Deprivation of Life and other Unlawful or Politically Motivated Killings

There were several reports the government committed arbitrary or unlawful killings, representing a slight increase compared with the previous year.

Local human rights observers and Muslim community members expressed concern regarding police killings of Muslims under questionable circumstances. For example, on January 23, the Rwanda National Police (RNP) shot and killed Muslim Imam Mohamed Mugemangango while he was in custody. The RNP reported Mugemangango was trying to escape while in transit from his residence to the Kanombe police station. On August 19, RNP officers shot and killed three other Muslim community members in Bugarama. The RNP reported the three were trying to escape after resisting arrest. This incident came two days after the RNP in Kigali shot and killed another Muslim, Channy Mbonigaba. The RNP reported Mbonigaba exchanged gunfire with police, injuring one officer. In all three cases, the RNP issued statements indicating they suspected the individuals of having links to foreign terrorist organizations.

On July 21, Human Rights Watch (HRW) reported it received information regarding several persons who died during or just after their detention in the Mudende detention center, reportedly due to a combination of injuries from beatings, poor conditions, and lack of medical care.

The African Union (AU) pressed the governments of Rwanda and Burundi to follow through on their publicly stated support for an AU-led investigation into the 2014 discovery of corpses in Lake Rweru, which spans the border between the two countries, but no investigation commenced by year's end. The government maintained the bodies appeared on the Burundi side of the border and insisted that any investigation of the incident must commence in Burundi.

b. Disappearance

In contrast with the previous year, there were several reports of politically motivated disappearances during the year.

On March 26, Illuminee Iragena, a member of the unregistered United Democratic Forces (FDU)-Inkingi party, disappeared, and there were unconfirmed reports she was killed while in SSF detention. The government had not initiated an investigation into her disappearance by year's end.

On August 7, journalist John Ndabarasa disappeared. Ndabarasa is the brother-in-law of Joel Mutabazi, a former bodyguard to the president, who was convicted of eight charges, including terrorism and treason, and sentenced to life in prison in 2014 after being deported from Uganda, a move condemned by the UN High Commissioner for Refugees (UNHCR), HRW, and Amnesty International as a violation of the principle of nonrefoulement. The RNP opened an investigation into Ndabarasa's disappearance and immediately issued a statement suggesting he had departed the country. Ndabarasa's family members and domestic human rights groups disputed this claim.

Domestic organizations critical of the SSF reported interference in their operations by the government and cited a lack of capacity and independence to investigate security-sector abuses.

c. Torture and Other Cruel, Inhuman, or Degrading Treatment or Punishment

The constitution and law prohibit such practices, but there were numerous reports of abuse of detainees and prisoners by police, military, and National Intelligence and Security Services (NISS) officials.

In 2012 the government signed into law a penal code that upgrades torture from an aggravating circumstance to a crime in itself. The law mandates the maximum penalty, defined by the extent of injury, for SSF and other government perpetrators. In 2014 the government ratified and indigenized the Optional Protocol to the Convention Against Torture.

There were reports military intelligence personnel and the SSF employed torture and other cruel, inhuman, or degrading treatment or punishment to obtain confessions in military detention centers. There were no reported prosecutions of SSF personnel for torture.

There were numerous reports police at times beat newly arrested suspects to obtain confessions. Allegations of abuse were particularly frequent at the police station in Gisenyi, located across the border from Goma in the Democratic Republic of the Congo (DRC). Official reports of sexual abuse were rare, but according to former detainees, transactional sex in prisons and detention centers occurred regularly.

In 2015 HRW and domestic observers reported the abuse of detained street vendors, persons in prostitution, and beggars at the Gikondo Transit Center, a detention facility in Kigali (locally known as "Kwa Kabuga"), by police and other detainees. The government disputed HRW's findings, denying the existence of undeclared detention centers and referring to Gikondo as a rehabilitation facility designed to provide "social emergency assistance" in lieu of incarceration. In November 2015 the Kigali City Council published guidelines for improving conditions at Gikondo, but the directives were vague and permitted arbitrary and lengthy detention. A July 21 follow-up report by HRW noted conditions at Gikondo improved only marginally and documented abuses at so-called transit centers in Muhanga, Mbazi, and Mudende. Former detainees reported routine and arbitrary beatings by police and other detainees, often with sticks. HRW interviews with prisoners and former detainees indicated inmates, acting under direction of detention center authorities, carried out a majority of beatings. According to HRW, several persons died during or just after their detention in Mudende.

Three RNP officers serving in the UN Stabilization Mission in Haiti were cited in a February 16 report by the UN secretary-general on sexual exploitation and abuse of civilians by international peacekeepers. All three were paternity cases arising from inappropriate relationships with adult victims. On March 4, the same day the United Nations released its report publicly, the government suspended the officers and opened investigations into their conduct, promising appropriate disciplinary action. The investigations had not concluded by year's end.

Prison and Detention Center Conditions

Prison conditions ranged from harsh and life threatening to meeting international standards. The government took steps to improve conditions in some prisons and constructed additional facilities to relieve overcrowding, but conditions varied widely among prisons.

Domestic civil society organizations reported impediments for persons with disabilities, including lack of sign language interpreters at police stations and detention centers.

<u>Physical Conditions</u>: According to the Rwanda Correctional Service (RCS), the prison population steadily declined from 58,515 in 2011 to 53,600 in 2014. It was expected to decline further in the coming years as convicted persons sentenced to

20-25 years' imprisonment for crimes related to the 1994 genocide, who comprised approximately 60 percent of the prison population, finished serving their sentences.

Conditions were generally worse and often harsh and life threatening in detention and transit centers. In July, HRW reported that, according to former detainees, upwards of 200-400 men, women, and children were detained at any one time in each of the Mbazi, Muhanga, and Mudende transit centers, while the number of detainees in Gikondo ranged from 200 to 800 persons, who were held in several large rooms. HRW reports suggested similar conditions prevailed in other transit and detention centers, of which there were at least 28 across the country.

Authorities held men and women separately in similar conditions, although overcrowding was more prevalent in men's wards.

Detention centers in general lacked separate facilities for children. According to HRW, officials held children together with adults in Muhanga, Mudende, and Gikondo. They sometimes held minors in separate facilities, as in Mbazi, that had marginally better conditions than the facilities for adults. There was also a minors-only facility in Nyagatare; observers reported Nyagatare came close to meeting international norms and noted authorities provided children detained there with formal education opportunities.

According to the Ministry of Justice, 152 children under age three lived with their mothers in prison. The law does not allow children over the age of three to remain with their incarcerated mothers.

Authorities generally separated pretrial detainees from convicted prisoners, although there were numerous exceptions due to the large number of detainees awaiting trial.

The government held six prisoners of the Special Court for Sierra Leone in a purpose-built detention center that the United Nations deemed met international standards for incarceration of prisoners convicted by international criminal tribunals. The government held international transfers and some high-profile "security" prisoners in similarly upgraded maximum-security wings of Kigali Central "1930" Prison.

Prisoner deaths resulted from anemia, HIV/AIDS, respiratory diseases, malaria, and other diseases at rates similar to those found in the general population. Medical care in prisons was commensurate with care for the public at large, because the government enrolled all prisoners in the national health insurance plan. Prisoners were fed once per day, but there were no provisions for feeding those in pretrial detention, who relied on family members for food. Authorities permitted family members to supplement the diets of vulnerable prisoners with health problems. HRW stated several detainees shared mattresses that were often infested with lice and fleas. According to HRW, the government upgraded the Gikondo Transit Center, including improvements to toilets and other sanitation facilities, but conditions still fell short of international standards. There were reports of improvements to heating, ventilation, and lighting in prisons in the local media; however, the reports did not mention specific details of upgrades or measures implemented by the government.

Conditions in police and military detention centers varied. Overcrowding was common in police stations and detention centers, and poor ventilation often led to high temperatures. Provision of adequate food and medical care was inconsistent.

Authorities transferred transit center male detainees and at-risk adults ages 18 to 35 to the Iwawa Rehabilitation and Vocational Development Center on Iwawa Island in Lake Kivu. Sanitation, nutrition, and health services at the center generally met international standards.

<u>Administration</u>: Recordkeeping on prisoners and detainees remained inadequate. Domestic and international human rights organizations reported instances of long delays and failures to locate prisoners and detainees. In January authorities implemented a pilot integrated electronic case management system (IECMS); domestic observers praised IECMS's potential to improve accountability and transparency in record keeping, but they noted it also created substantial barriers in access to justice in rural areas where lack of computers, internet, electricity, and technological knowledge prevented many from accessing IECMS.

In January the Ministry of Justice announced the completion of its investigation into the cases of 7,099 prisoners convicted of genocide and related crimes by traditional gacaca (community-based) courts who claimed they were kept in prison beyond their sentences. The Justice Ministry-led commission, which included the RCS, Ministry of Internal Security, and National Human Rights Commission (NHRC), stated it found no basis for the prisoners' claims but noted shoddy record keeping and corruption among RCS personnel led to an increasing number of incomplete prisoner files. A Ministry of Justice spokesperson said most of the concerned prisoners appeared to have bribed RCS officials to remove their sentencing decrees from their prison files, thereby creating confusion regarding the lengths of their sentences. Although the commission found that none of the prisoners merited release, it instructed the RCS to respect fully the prisoners' rights. The commission did not make its final report public, and prisoners continued making appeals to the NHRC to have their cases reviewed.

In 2013 the government disarmed approximately 770 March 23 Movement Congolese rebel combatants who crossed into the country from the DRC and detained them in a converted police training facility in Ngoma. As in previous years, detainees left or escaped the Ngoma internment center, and the government was unable to account for their whereabouts. In September observers reported there were approximately 100 detainees in the internment center, a substantial decrease from the nearly 400 individuals interned in the center at the end of 2015; 29 of the former combatants were positively identified among the refugee population in the country's five Congolese camps.

The RCS investigated reported abuses by corrections officers, and the same hierarchical structure existed in police and security forces; there was no independent institution charged with investigating abuses or punishing perpetrators.

Detainees held at the Iwawa Rehabilitation and Vocational Development Center did not have the right to appeal their detentions to judicial authorities.

Independent Monitoring: The government permitted independent monitoring of prison conditions on a limited basis by diplomats and the International Committee of the Red Cross. At times, however, it restricted access to specific prisoners and did not permit monitors to visit undeclared detention centers and certain military intelligence facilities. The government effectively barred HRW from conducting research inside the country after the publication of HRW's 2015 and 2016 reports on the Gikondo Transit Center. A limited number of local NGOs were supposedly permitted to monitor prison conditions but did not do so, citing intimidation by the government.

Journalists could access prisons with a valid press card but required permission from the RCS commissioner to take photographs or interview prisoners or guards.

Improvements: According to the Legal Aid Forum, which provided legal assistance to inmates, there were improvements in the treatment of the general prison population, including the organization of "legal aid week" events, the appointment of legal officers in every prison, and the dedication of the Ngoma prison exclusively for women. Under its strategic plan for 2013-18, the RCS built a prison in the Mageragere suburb of Kigali to relieve overcrowding in the Kigali Central "1930" and Kimironko prisons.

d. Arbitrary Arrest or Detention

The constitution and law prohibit arbitrary arrest and detention, but SSF personnel regularly arrested and detained persons arbitrarily and without due process.

Domestic observers reported the RNP systematically rounded up and arbitrarily detained street children, street vendors, suspected drug abusers, persons in prostitution, homeless persons, suspected petty criminals, and suspected serious offenders ahead of the AU Summit, held in Kigali July 10-18. As in previous years, they held detainees without charge at the Gikondo Transit Center before transferring them to the Iwawa Rehabilitation and Vocational Development Center without judicial review. The government maintained that individuals in transit and rehabilitation centers were not detainees, although they could not leave the centers.

Unregistered opposition political parties reported authorities frequently arrested their supporters and party officials but released most after detention of one week or less, although several, including FDU-Inkingi assistant secretary Leonille Gasengayire, completed longer detention. On August 23, police arrested Gasengayire for inciting the public against the public order, and he remained in detention at year's end. The charge stemmed from meetings Gasengayire allegedly organized in which she urged residents of Rutsiro District in Western Province to resist forcible relocation after expropriation of their land holdings for the construction of government buildings. Domestic and international observers disputed the prosecution's claim and argued political considerations motivated the charges.

In May authorities detained retired colonel Ben Karenzi, who served as director of the RDF's Kanombe military hospital, for traveling outside the country without authorization. Authorities also detained several other high-ranking military officials for facilitating Kanombe's trip to Nairobi in April but subsequently released them without filing charges. Karenzi remained in detention and had neither been charged with a crime nor appeared in civilian or military court by year's end.

Role of the Police and Security Apparatus

The RNP, moved to the Ministry of Justice after the dissolution of the Ministry of Internal Security in October, is responsible for internal security. The RDF, under the Ministry of Defense, is in charge of providing external security, although the RDF also works on internal security and intelligence matters alongside the RNP. In December the cabinet approved the creation of the Rwanda Investigation Bureau under the Ministry of Justice. The decision effectively removes responsibility for investigations and prosecutions from the RNP and vests it with the newly created bureau.

Civilian authorities generally maintained control over the RNP and the RDF, and the government had mechanisms to investigate and punish abuse and corruption. The Inspectorate General of the RNP generally disciplined police for excessive use of force and prosecuted acts of corruption. Nevertheless, there were reports elements of the SSF at times acted independently of civilian control. For example, there were reports RDF J-2 (intelligence staff), NISS, and RNP intelligence personnel were responsible for disappearances, illegal detention, and torture in military and police detention centers, both declared and undeclared.

The RDF normally displayed a high level of military professionalism and discipline. In September, RDF Major Aimable Rugomwa shot and killed a young boy in Kanombe on suspicion of theft. Authorities immediately arrested Rugomwa and charged him with murder, and a military tribunal refused him bail. The RDF High Command visited the deceased boy's family and issued a communique denouncing the officer.

Police at times lacked sufficient basic resources--such as handcuffs, radios, and patrol cars--but observers credited the RNP with generally strong discipline and effectiveness. The RNP institutionalized community relations training that included appropriate use of force and human rights, although arbitrary arrests and beatings remained problems.

There were reports of abuse of suspects by the District Administration Security Support Organ (DASSO), including the May 7 killing of a street vendor in Kigali during a DASSO patrol. Police arrested the perpetrator and charged him with murder, and the incident prompted authorities to organize human rights training for all DASSO personnel, who numbered approximately 2,600.

Arrest Procedures and Treatment of Detainees

The law requires authorities to investigate and obtain a warrant before arresting a suspect. Police may detain suspects for up to 72 hours without an arrest warrant. Prosecutors must submit formal charges within five days of arrest. Police may detain minors a maximum of 15 days in pretrial detention, but only for crimes that carry a penalty for conviction of five years' or more imprisonment. There were numerous reports police and prosecutors disregarded these provisions and held individuals, sometimes for months and often without charge, particularly in security-related cases. The SSF held some suspects incommunicado or under house arrest. At times police employed nonjudicial punishment when minor criminals confessed and the victims agreed to the police officer's recommended penalty, such as a week of detention or restitution.

The law permits investigative detention if authorities believe public safety is threatened or the accused might flee, and judges interpreted these provisions broadly, as in the cases of 28 arrested Rwandan Muslims--17 in January, three in May, three in July, and five in August--accused of religious radicalism and suspected of collaboration with international terrorist groups whose trial had not commenced by year's end. A judge must review such detention every 30 days, and it may not extend beyond one year, but the SSF held numerous suspects indefinitely after the first authorization of investigative detention and did not always seek reauthorization every 30 days.

After prosecutors formally file a charge, detention may be indefinite unless bail is granted. Bail exists only for crimes for which the maximum sentence if convicted is five years' imprisonment, but authorities may release a suspect pending trial if satisfied the person would not flee or become a threat to public safety and order. Authorities generally allowed family members prompt access to detained relatives, unless the individuals were held on state security charges, at intelligence-related detention centers such as Camp Kami or Kwa Gacinya, or in undeclared detention facilities. The government at times violated the right to habeas corpus.

By law detainees are allowed access to lawyers, but the scarcity of lawyers and their reluctance to take on cases that were considered sensitive for political or state security reasons limited access to legal representation. Some lawyers working on politically sensitive cases reported harassment and threats by government officials and denial of access to the evidence against their clients.

During a 2014 RDF and RNP security operation in Musanze and Rubavu, the SSF detained persons incommunicado without access to legal representation for up to two months. The SSF released numerous individuals without charge; however, the government charged 77 persons with crimes against state security, including collaborating with the rebel group Democratic Forces for the Liberation of Rwanda. Judges ordered the release of 33 of the 77 in 2014, while upholding charges against 44 in pretrial hearing. In 2015, six defendants were convicted and sentenced to life in prison, five were sentenced to 10-year prison terms, and three were acquitted. Local human rights organizations reported the defendants did not have legal counsel. Trials of other defendants continued at year's end.

Convicted persons sometimes remained in prison after completing their sentences while waiting for an appeal date or due to problems with prison records. The law provides that pretrial detention, illegal detention, and administrative sanctions be fully deducted from sentences imposed, but it does not provide for compensation to persons who are acquitted. The law allows judges to impose detention of equivalent duration and fines on SSF and other government officials who unlawfully detained individuals, but there were no reports that judges exercised this authority.

Arbitrary Arrest: Unregistered opposition parties claimed police at times arbitrarily arrested their members (see section 3).

Although there is no requirement for individuals to carry identification, police and the DASSO regularly detained street children, vendors, and beggars without identification and sometimes charged them with illegal street vending or vagrancy. Authorities released adults who could produce identification and transported street children to their home districts, to shelters, or for processing into vocational and educational programs.

There were numerous reports authorities detained family members of individuals suspected of committing crimes if the suspects themselves could not be located. Authorities advertised the detention of the suspects' relatives but released them without charges if the suspects turned themselves in.

Pretrial Detention: Lengthy pretrial detention was a serious problem. The NHRC reported to parliament in 2013 that authorities often detained prisoners for extended periods without arraignment, and domestic and international human rights organizations reported the practice continued during the year. The law permits detention of genocide suspects until trial. Authorities permitted the majority of convicted prisoners (those who confessed their genocide crimes) to return to their families, with prison time to be served after the suspended and community service portions of their sentences.

The government made strides toward eliminating the case backlog and reducing the average length of pretrial detention. The government and the Legal Aid Forum trained paralegals and Mediation Committees (Abunzi) mediators to handle minor civil cases through alternate dispute mechanisms outside the court system. In 2015 the government promulgated national regulations on the organization, jurisdiction, competence, and functioning of cell- and sector-level mediation committees, whose members were elected locally, expanding their jurisdiction to include criminal cases. If one of the parties to a dispute rejected the sector-level mediation committee's decision, they could appeal it to the local primary court.

The inspector general of the National Public Prosecution Authority (NPPA) sanctioned government officials who abused regulations on pretrial detention with penalties, including fines and suspensions.

Detainee's Ability to Challenge Lawfulness of Detention before a Court: Although detainees have the right to challenge their detention in court, few tried and none were able to obtain prompt release or compensation for unlawful detention.

e. Denial of Fair Public Trial

The constitution and law provide for an independent judiciary, and the judiciary operated in most cases without government interference. As in previous years, there were no reports of direct government interference in the judiciary, and authorities generally respected court orders. Domestic observers noted, however, that outcomes in high-profile trials of genocide suspects and military leaders accused of inciting rebellion appeared predetermined.

Trial Procedures

The law provides for a presumption of innocence. The law requires defendants be informed promptly and in detail of the charges in a language they comprehend.

Defendants have the right to a fair trial without undue delay. In its 2015-16 activity report, the NPPA stated it had processed to conclusion 91 percent of the 18,484 cases it had received, just short of its 97 percent target. Despite the NPPA's conclusion that its 181 prosecutors handled all cases without significant undue delay, defense lawyers reported there were an insufficient number of prosecutors, judges, and courtrooms to hold trials within a reasonable time.

Defendants have the right to communicate with an attorney of their choice, although many defendants could not afford private counsel. The law provides for legal representation of minors. The law does not provide for an attorney at state expense for indigent defendants. The Rwandan Bar Association and 36 other member organizations of the Legal Aid Forum provided legal assistance to some indigent defendants but lacked the resources to provide defense counsel to all in need. Legal aid organizations noted the requirement that defendants present a certificate of indigence signed by their village chief made it difficult to qualify for pro bono representation. Domestic organizations working to expand access to justice noted that a substantial increase in court fees implemented in conjunction with the IECMS rollout posed significant additional barriers for poor defendants.

The law requires that defendants have adequate time and facilities to prepare their defense, and judges routinely granted requests to extend preparation time. The law provides for a right to free interpretation, but domestic human rights organizations noted officials did not always enforce this right, particularly in cases of deaf and hard of hearing defendants requiring sign language interpreters. Defendants and their attorneys have the right to access government-held evidence relevant to their cases, but courts and prosecutors did not always respect this right. Defendants have the right to be present at trial, confront witnesses against them, and present witnesses and evidence on their own behalf. By law defendants may not be compelled to testify or confess guilt, and judges generally respected the law during trial. The law provides for the right to appeal, and authorities respected this provision.

There were some reports the SSF coerced suspects into confessing guilt in security-related cases. Judges tended to accept confessions obtained through torture despite defendants' protests and failed to order investigations when defendants alleged torture during their trial (see section on political prisoners below). There were fewer such cases during the year compared with previous years.

The RDF routinely tried military offenders and civilians who previously served in the RDF before military tribunals that rendered penalties of fines, imprisonment, or both. Military courts provided defendants with similar rights as civilian courts, including the right of appeal and access to government-held evidence relevant to their cases. Defendants often appeared before military tribunals without legal counsel due to the cost of hiring private attorneys and the unwillingness of some attorneys to defend individuals accused of crimes against state security. The law stipulates military courts may try civilian accomplices of soldiers accused of crimes. The government did not release figures on the number of civilians tried as coperpetrators or accomplices of military personnel.

In 2012 the International Criminal Tribunal for Rwanda transferred its remaining genocide cases to a Tanzania-based branch of the Mechanism for International Criminal Tribunals. It continued to pursue genocide fugitives subject to Rwanda tribunal indictments, and in March the former mayor of Nyakizu, Ladislas Ntaganzwa, was extradited to Rwanda from the DRC. Ntaganzwa was one of nine major genocide suspects who had remained at large.

Political Prisoners and Detainees

There were numerous reports local officials and the SSF briefly detained some individuals who disagreed publicly with government decisions or policies. Opposition leaders and government critics faced indictment under broadly applied charges of genocide incitement, genocide denial, divisionism, and incitement to rebel. Numerous individuals identified by international and domestic human rights groups as political prisoners remained in prison, including Victoire Ingabire, Deo Mushayidi, and Theoneste Niyitegeka.

President of the FDU-Inkingi and former 2010 presidential candidate Victoire Ingabire was sentenced to eight years' imprisonment in 2012 in what was considered a flawed trial based on politically motivated charges. In February, ahead of Ingabire's appeal before the African Court on Human and People's Rights (ACHPR), her lawyer claimed officials denied him access to Ingabire and stated authorities had demanded to see all documents he intended to bring to prison to discuss with his client. In September a visiting delegation from the EU Parliament was denied access to Ingabire, who is a Dutch citizen; an RCS spokesperson claimed the government had not received an official request for the visit.

Convicted and sentenced to 15 years' imprisonment in 2008 for complicity in genocide, former 2003 presidential candidate Theoneste Niyitegeka remained in prison at year's end. International and domestic human rights organizations claimed the charges against Niyitegeka were politically motivated and that there were serious irregularities in Niyitegeka's appeal proceedings in sector-level courts.

On March 31, the Military High Court of Kanombe sentenced Colonel Tom Byabagamba and retired brigadier general Frank Rusagara to 21 and 20 years' imprisonment, respectively, for inciting insurrection and tarnishing the government's image. The court sentenced Rusagara's driver, Francois Kabayiza, to five years' imprisonment for concealing evidence. Kabayiza said in court military personnel tortured him in detention, but the judges in the case did not order an investigation into his allegations, stating he lacked proof he was tortured. HRW documented numerous irregularities in these two cases, including the fact judges allowed the defense to cross-examine only four of the 11 prosecution witnesses. One of these, retired captain David Kabuye, was arrested at approximately the same time; Kabuye stated during his own trial he was forced to testify against Rusagara and Byabagamba.

Civil Judicial Procedures and Remedies

The judiciary was generally independent and impartial in civil matters. Mechanisms exist for citizens to file lawsuits in civil matters, including for violations of human rights. The Office of the Ombudsman processed claims of judicial wrongdoing on an administrative basis.

In March, days before the ACHPR was set to hear an appeal by Victoire Ingabire, the government withdrew from the additional ACHPR protocol that allows individuals and organizations to challenge adverse domestic decisions before the court. Individuals may still submit cases to the East African Court of Justice (EACJ).

Property Restitution

Reports of expropriation of land for the construction of roads, government buildings, and other infrastructure projects were common, and complainants frequently cited government failure to provide adequate and timely compensation. The NCHR investigated these cases and advocated on citizens' behalf with relevant local and national authorities but was unable to effect restitution in a majority of the cases.

In September the First Instance Division of the EACJ began hearings in the case of Tribert Rujugiro Ayabatwa, a Rwandan businessperson living in self-imposed exile in South Africa whose United Trade Center shopping mall in Kigali, valued at 16.2 billion Rwandan francs ($20 million), was seized by the government in 2013. In 2014 the EACJ appellate division ordered a rehearing of the case, citing irregularities in the original decision.

The government did not provide an update on the case of Assinapol Rwigara, whose family claimed the SSF killed Rwigara after an automobile accident in February 2015. Following Rwigara's death, Kigali municipal authorities seized real estate owned by him, and in September 2015 demolished a hotel belonging to the Rwigara family. The authorities claimed the hotel was built without proper permits and was structurally unsound; the family disputed the claim and provided copies of building permits to the press. The family claimed the government and City of Kigali did not provide compensation for the loss of property and investment. During the year the family further claimed authorities threatened to close and repossess several factories belonging to the family.

f. Arbitrary or Unlawful Interference with Privacy, Family, Home, or Correspondence

Although the constitution and law prohibit such actions, there were numerous reports the government monitored homes, movements, telephone calls, e-mail, other private communications, and personal and institutional data. There were reports of government informants working within international and local NGOs, religious organizations, and other social institutions.

The law requires police to obtain authorization from a state prosecutor prior to entering and searching citizens' homes. According to human rights organizations, the SSF at times entered homes without obtaining the required authorization.

The penal code provides legal protection against unauthorized use of personal data by private entities, although officials did not invoke these provisions during the year.

RPF members regularly visited citizens' homes seeking contributions to the political party and the government's Agaciro Development Fund, established by the government in 2012 to accelerate the country's independence from international aid.

Section 2. Respect for Civil Liberties, Including:

a. Freedom of Speech and Press

The constitution provides for freedom of speech and press "in conditions prescribed by the law," but the government severely restricted these rights.

Journalists reported government officials questioned, threatened, and at times arrested journalists who expressed views deemed critical on sensitive topics.

The Rwanda Media Commission (RMC), a self-regulatory body, sometimes intervened on journalists' behalf, as it did in the August disappearance of journalist John Ndabarasa. The RMC also remonstrated against the attack on a foreign journalist, who was injured by a DASSO officer while covering a DASSO operation in May. Journalists also reported the RMC lost its independence following the May 2015 ouster and subsequent exile of its elected chairperson Fred Muvunyi.

Freedom of Speech and Expression: There were no official restrictions on individuals' right to criticize the government publicly or privately on policy implementation and other issues. Nonetheless, the government generally did not tolerate criticism of the presidency and government policy on security and other matters that were deemed sensitive. For example, in February the RNP detained two journalists who were preparing a report on tax evasion involving the country's main stone quarry. After their release, the journalists recounted how members of the RMC accompanied the RNP officers who searched and confiscated computers and various files before detaining them.

Laws prohibiting divisionism, genocide ideology, and genocide denial discouraged citizens from expressing viewpoints some might construe as promoting societal divisions. The law prohibits the propagation of ideas based on "ethnic, regional, racial, religious, language, or other divisive characteristics." Conviction of public incitement to "genocide ideology" or "divisionism," including discrimination and sectarianism, is punishable by five to nine years' imprisonment and fines of 100,000 to one million Rwandan francs ($123 to $1,234). Authorities applied the laws broadly, including to silence political dissent and to shut down investigative journalism.

The 2012 penal code expanded former provisions that prohibited the display of contempt for the head of state or other high-level public officials to include administrative authorities or other public servants, with sentences of one to two years' imprisonment and fines of 50,000 to 500,000 Rwandan francs ($61 to $617). Other changes included revising the crime of "spreading rumors aimed at inciting the population to rise against the regime" to "spreading false information with intent to create a hostile international opinion against the Rwandan state," with much more severe penalties, including life in prison for conviction for acts committed during wartime and seven to 10 years' imprisonment for acts committed in peacetime. Slander and libel of foreign and international officials and dignitaries are illegal, with sentences of one to three years' imprisonment.

In 2013 the government signed into law a revised genocide ideology law that introduced international definitions for genocide and narrowed the scope of what constitutes "genocide ideology" and related offenses to a more specific range of actions and statements. Specifically, the law states that "genocidal ideology" must be clearly linked to specific acts or statements, rather than the broader "aggregate of thoughts" standard defined in the 2008 law. Nevertheless, authorities applied the statute broadly, and there were numerous reports of its use to silence persons critical of government policy.

The government investigated and prosecuted individuals accused of threatening or harming genocide survivors and witnesses or of espousing genocide ideology, which the law defines as dehumanizing an individual or a group with the same characteristics by threatening, intimidating, defaming, inciting hatred, denying the genocide, taking revenge, altering testimony or evidence, killing, planning to kill, or attempting to kill someone.

Prosecutions for genocide ideology and genocide denial rose from 20 reported cases between October 2014 and September 2015 to 78 cases from October 2015 to September; however, it still fell well short of the nearly 800 cases handled by the NPPA in 2012-13. According to the NPPA, 69 cases were prosecuted to completion, two were dropped, and seven remained pending at year's end.

<u>Press and Media Freedoms</u>: Vendors sold both private and government-owned newspapers published in English, French, and Kinyarwanda. There were 53 newspapers, journals, and other publications registered with the government, although fewer than 10 published regularly. Sporadically published independent newspapers maintained positions both in support of and contrary to or critical of the government. There were 33 radio stations (six government-owned and 27 independent), one government-run television station, and five independent television stations. Independent media reported a difficult operating environment and highlighted the reluctance of the business community to advertise on radio stations that might be critical of the government, leading one such station to suspend operations. An independently published newspaper that was sometimes critical of the government cited similar reasons in announcing its closure in December.

A set of five media laws passed in 2013 provide for greater press freedoms but had no discernable effect on those freedoms. Despite the reforms, media professionals reported government officials sought to influence reporting and warned journalists against reporting information deemed sensitive or critical of the government. The board of the RMC was reconstituted following the May 2015 resignation of Chairman Fred Muvunyi. Journalists reported all positions on the RMC board were filled in close consultation with the government and the board hewed closely to RPF orthodoxy. Journalists also said the December election of the new RMC board violated the RMC's bylaws.

The laws provide journalists the freedom to investigate, express opinions, and "seek, receive, give, and broadcast information and ideas through any media." The law explicitly prohibits censorship of information, but censorship occurred. The laws restrict these freedoms if journalists "jeopardize the general public order and good morals, an individual's right to honor and reputation in the public eye and to the right to inviolability of a person's private life and family." Authorities may seize journalists' material and information if a "media offense" occurs but only if a court orders it. Authorities sometimes seized journalists' material without a court order. Courts may compel journalists to reveal confidential sources in the event of an investigation or criminal proceeding. Persons wanting to start a media outlet must apply with the "competent public organ." All media rights and prohibitions apply to persons writing for websites.

<u>Violence and Harassment</u>: There were reports police and the SSF at times detained and harassed journalists. In January police arrested reporter John Williams Ntwari and charged him with raping a minor. Prior to the arrest, Ntwari reported receiving threats for his coverage of the Rwigara death and expropriation case. Officials released Ntwari after 10 days when other journalists interviewed the alleged victim and discovered that she was not a minor and there was no evidence of use of force.

Several journalists who fled in prior years remained outside the country, including former RMC chairman Fred Muvunyi, who went into self-exile after arguing against the government's call to ban the BBC's Kinyarwanda service following the broadcast of a BBC documentary, which was controversial in the country.

<u>Censorship or Content Restrictions</u>: The law allows the government to restrict access to some government documents and information, including information on individual privacy and information or statements deemed to constitute defamation. Journalists reported editorial boards for major print and broadcast media

companies censored information deemed critical of the RPF or government policies.

Radio stations broadcast criticism of government policies, including on popular citizen call-in shows; however, journalists reported self-censorship and were careful to distance themselves from opinions expressed by call-in guests that could be deemed controversial. Some radio stations, including Radio 1, Radio Isango Star, and Radio Salus, had regular call-in shows that featured discussion of government programs or policies. Several radio stations hosted live debates on sensitive topics, such as power sharing after the 2017 presidential elections.

Libel/Slander Laws: Conviction of defamation (libel and slander) is a criminal offense punishable by fines and imprisonment. There were no reports of slander and libel laws being used to suppress freedom of speech or the publication of material that criticized government policies or government officials.

National Security: Under the 2013 media laws, journalists must refrain from reporting items that violate "confidentiality in the national security and national integrity" and "confidentiality of judicial proceedings, parliamentary sessions, and cabinet deliberations in camera." Authorities invoked these laws to arrest and intimidate journalists covering politically sensitive topics and matters under government investigation.

Internet Freedom

The media law includes the right of all citizens to "receive, disseminate, or send information through internet," including the right to start and maintain a website. All provisions of the media laws apply to web-based publications. Restrictions such as website blocking remained in place, however. There were numerous reports the government monitored e-mail and internet chat rooms. Individuals and groups could engage in the peaceful expression of views via the internet, including by e-mail and social media, but were subject to monitoring. As in the previous year, there were no confirmed reports monitoring led to detention or interrogation of individuals by the SSF. According to the International Telecommunication Union, 18 percent of the population used the internet in 2015.

Government-run social media accounts were used to debate and at times intimidate individuals who posted online comments considered critical of the government.

The government blocked access within the country to several websites critical of its policies. Such sites included websites of the Rwandan diaspora such as *Umuvugizi* and *Le Profete* and online newspapers such as *Ireme.com*.

Academic Freedom and Cultural Events

The government generally did not restrict academic freedom or cultural events, but because academic officials frequently suspended outspoken secondary and university students for divisionism or engaging in genocide ideology, students and professors practiced self-censorship. Local think tanks deferred to government officials in selecting subjects for research, and authorities sometimes prevented the publication of studies that cast the government in a negative light. The government requires visiting academics to receive official permission to conduct research; academics reported occasional harassment and denial of permission to conduct research on political issues, refugees, or the genocide.

b. Freedom of Peaceful Assembly and Association

Freedom of Assembly

The constitution and law provide for freedom of assembly, but the government did not always respect this right. In 2014 the UN special rapporteur on the rights to freedom of assembly and association, Maina Kiai, reported, "peaceful protests voicing dissent and criticizing government policies are reportedly not allowed."

Authorities may legally require advance notice for public meetings and demonstrations and must respond to notification within one week or 15 days, depending on the type of event. Even with prior written authorization, public meetings were subject to disruption or arbitrary closure. For example, during the July AU Summit, police prevented local human rights organizations from organizing a press conference with their regional counterparts. The conference organizers obtained authorization from relevant ministries well in advance of the event, but RNP officers forcefully dispersed the participants and prevented the event from taking place.

Freedom of Association

While the constitution provides for freedom of association, the government limited the right. The law requires private organizations to register. Although the government generally granted licenses, it impeded the formation of new political parties, restricted political party activities, and delayed or denied registration to local and international NGOs seeking to work on human rights, media freedom, or political advocacy (see section 3). In addition the government imposed difficult and burdensome NGO registration and renewal requirements, especially on international NGOs, as well as time-consuming requirements for annual financial and activity reports (see section 5).

c. Freedom of Religion

See the Department of State's *International Religious Freedom Report* at www.state.gov/religiousfreedomreport/.

d. Freedom of Movement, Internally Displaced Persons, Protection of Refugees, and Stateless Persons

The constitution and law provide for freedom of internal movement, foreign travel, emigration, and repatriation, and the government generally respected these rights.

The government cooperated with UNHCR and other humanitarian organizations in providing protection and assistance to internally displaced persons, refugees, returning refugees, asylum seekers, stateless persons, and other persons of concern. The government granted prima facie refugee status to Burundian refugees fleeing instability after Burundi's 2015 presidential election. In 2015 to November 7, more than 81,600 Burundian refugees entered the country, joining approximately 74,000 Congolese refugees who had sought refuge between 1994 and 2015.

UNHCR administered Mahama camp for Burundian refugees and five camps primarily for Congolese refugees with international NGOs, providing for basic health, water, sanitation, housing, feeding, and educational needs. Authorities sometimes restricted access to the camps. In June the government issued new instructions on camp management clarifying procedures for requesting access to the camps. Following the promulgation of these instructions, UNHCR reported excellent cooperation with the government and local community. In addition to increasing integration of refugees into the national education and health-care systems, the government also cooperated with UNHCR to launch a livelihoods strategy in September focused on increasing refugees' economic integration.

UNHCR recommended that countries invoke the "ceased circumstances" clause for Rwandans who fled the country between 1959 and 1998. During the year UNHCR extended the agreement with African states hosting Rwandan refugees that refugees are to be assisted in returning to Rwanda or obtaining legal permanent residency in host countries by December 31, 2017. The cessation clause forms part of the 1951 Refugee Convention and may be applied when fundamental and durable changes in a refugee's country of origin, such that they no longer have a well-founded fear of persecution, remove the need for international protection. Both UNHCR and the government agreed that since the end of the civil war and the 1994 genocide, the country had been peaceful, and more than three million exiled Rwandans had returned, including 5,082 during the year.

Foreign Travel: The law allows a judge to deprive convicted persons of the right to travel abroad as a stand-alone punishment or as punishment following imprisonment. Government officials must obtain written permission from the Office of the Prime Minister or the president before traveling abroad for official or personal reasons. The government restricted the travel of serving and former security-sector officials and arrested those who traveled abroad without authorization.

Members of the unregistered FDU-Inkingi party stated that authorities denied the issuance of or confiscated the passports of party members and their relatives.

Exile: The law prohibits forced exile. Some political dissidents, journalists, social activists, and former "security" detainees who claimed harassment and intimidation by the government left the country in previous years and remained in self-imposed exile. Some diplomatic personnel out of favor with the government failed to return upon conclusion of their assignments abroad.

Emigration and Repatriation: According to UNHCR, approximately 2,000 nationals returned from other countries during the year; most resettled in their districts of origin. The government worked with UNHCR and other aid organizations to assist the returnees.

The government interned former Congolese March 23 Movement combatants in a detention facility in Ngoma, but many former combatants continued to depart the facility during the year (see section 1.c., Prison and Detention Center Conditions).

The government accepted former Rwandan combatants who returned from the DRC. The Rwandan Demobilization and Reintegration Commission, with international support, placed adult former combatants in a three-month re-education program at Mutobo Demobilization Center in Northern Province. After completion, each adult former combatant was enrolled automatically in the RDF

Reserve Force and received 60,000 Rwandan francs ($74) and permission to return home. After two months each former combatant received an additional 120,000 Rwandan francs ($148). In November, 54 former combatants graduated from Mutobo, bringing the total number of reintegrated ex-combatants to approximately 200 for the year. The Musanze Child Rehabilitation Center, relocated in 2015 from Muhazi, Eastern Province, treated former child combatants in Northern Province.

Protection of Refugees

Authorities generally provided adequate security and physical protection within refugee camps. The RNP worked with UNHCR to build police posts on the edge of and station police officers in refugee camps. Refugees were free to file complaints at both camp and area police stations. Sexual and gender-based violence (GBV) was a problem, although formal reports of GBV in the camps declined precipitously during the year. UNHCR attributed the sharp decrease in reported GBV cases to a combination of increased GBV training of RNP officers at refugee camps, expanded NGO-run prevention and protection programs, and a pervasive culture of silence among refugee communities, who tended to underreport incidents of GBV.

In contrast to the previous year, there were no confirmed reports of recruitment of refugees into armed groups, and the government adopted stronger measures to protect vulnerable refugee populations residing in the country. The government, however, did not conduct a public investigation into credible allegations of recruitment of Burundian refugees, including children, from Mahama refugee camp between May and September 2015, and some refugees reported facing continued harassment and intimidation from authorities for their whistleblowing role in reporting recruitment.

Access to Asylum: The law provides for the granting of asylum or refugee status. UNHCR, with government and donor support, assisted approximately 165,000 refugees and asylum seekers, mostly from Burundi and the DRC. Of these, approximately 9,000 were Congolese asylum seekers who faced protracted delays in the adjudication of their asylum claims.

Human rights organizations reported that the government accepted asylum seekers of Eritrean and Sudanese origin deported from Israel to Rwanda and that many of the deportees subsequently were transported to Uganda. During the visit in July of Israeli Prime Minister Netanyahu, the president confirmed continuing discussions regarding cooperation between the two governments on this issue, but government officials declined to disclose the terms of any agreement.

<u>Freedom of Movement</u>: The law does not place restrictions on freedom of movement of asylum seekers, but refugees stated that delays in the issuance of identity cards and Convention Travel Documents (CTDs) restricted their ability to travel within and outside the country. The government committed to issuing all refugees identification cards and machine-readable CTDs upon the conclusion of a joint verification exercise with UNHCR. Verification was scheduled for October but had not commenced by year's end.

<u>Employment</u>: No laws restrict refugee employment, and in September the Ministry of Disaster Management and Refugee Affairs jointly launched a livelihoods strategy with UNHCR aimed at increasing the ability of refugees to work in the local economy. Officials acknowledged very few refugees were able to find local employment and offered periodic job training and livelihood programs to assist refugees in finding or creating income-generating opportunities. Refugees cited lack of government-issued identity documents as one of their main obstacles to employment.

<u>Access to Basic Services</u>: Refugees had access to public education through grade 10, public health care, housing within the refugee camps, law enforcement, courts and judicial procedures, and legal assistance. Refugees who arrived prior to 2013 were registered and provided with biometric identification cards similar to the national identity cards; however, there were significant delays in the issuance of identity documents to refugees who entered the country in 2013 and after. Refugees in the camps received basic health care and free treatment for more complicated cases through the national health insurance scheme. There were, however, approximately 30,000 Burundi-origin urban refugees residing in Kigali and Huye who could not access the national health insurance scheme. UNHCR and the government expanded access to secondary education beyond ninth grade and collaborated on increasing integrated learning opportunities. For example, UNHCR constructed a 112-classroom school in the village outside of Mahama camp--now the largest school in the country--that served more than 8,000 refugee students and 3,000 children from the host community in an integrated setting. Nevertheless, distance of some refugee camps from secondary schools and the cost of required school materials hindered access for some refugees.

<u>Durable Solutions</u>: The government did not accept refugees for resettlement. The government assisted the safe, voluntary return of refugees to their countries and

sought to improve local integration of refugees in protracted stays by permitting them to accept local employment and move freely in the country, and by establishing markets to facilitate trade between refugees and local citizens. The government did not facilitate the naturalization of refugees resident in the country.

Temporary Protection: The government provided temporary protection to individual asylum seekers who might not qualify as refugees.

Section 3. Freedom to Participate in the Political Process

The constitution and law provide citizens the ability to choose their government through free and fair elections based on universal and equal suffrage, but government restrictions on the formation of opposition parties limited that ability in practice. The law provides for voting by secret ballot in presidential and parliamentary--but not local--elections. The RPF and allied parties controlled the government and legislature, and its candidates dominated elections at all levels.

Elections and Political Participation

Recent Elections: Elections for parliament's lower house, the Chamber of Deputies, in 2013 were peaceful and orderly, but according to international observers did not meet the generally recognized standards for free and fair elections. In 2010 voters elected President Paul Kagame to a second seven-year term with 93 percent of the vote; the National Electoral Commission (NEC) reported that 97.5 percent of the population participated in the election. Observers' confidence in the integrity of electoral results was undermined by their being denied access to vote tabulation at the polling station, district, and national level. Opposition parties experienced difficulties in registering candidates ahead of the elections, depriving voters of a meaningful choice at the polls.

In 2015 the government held a constitutional referendum on a set of amendments that included provisions that would allow the president to run for up to three additional terms in office. The NEC reported 98 percent of registered voters participated, and 98 percent endorsed a set of amendments that retained term limits and included provisions that shorten the terms in office of the president and prime minister from seven years to five years but also provided an exception that would allow President Kagame to run for up to three additional terms in office (one seven-year term and up to two five-year terms). The text of the amendments was not generally available to voters for review prior to the referendum, and political parties opposed to the amendments were not permitted to hold rallies or public meetings to express their opposition to the amendments. Observers noted authorities strongly encouraged citizens to commit to supporting the amendments during "umuganda," the monthly mandatory day of community service. Independent international observers did not monitor or report on the conduct of the referendum.

<u>Political Parties and Political Participation</u>: The constitution outlines a multiparty system but provides few rights for parties and their candidates. There were some reports the RPF pressured youth into joining the party during mandatory "ingando" civic and military training camps after completing secondary school and "itorero" cultural school, which promoted patriotism in addition to inculcating national customs. There were also reports RPF members pressured teachers, clergy, and businesspersons to join the party and coerced political donations from both party members and nonmembers. Political parties allied to the RPF were largely able to operate freely, but members faced legal sanctions if found guilty of engaging in divisive acts, destabilizing national unity, threatening territorial integrity, or undermining national security.

The Democratic Green Party of Rwanda (DGPR) was registered officially as a political party in 2013, after the government blocked its attempts to register in 2009 and 2010. Authorities, however, granted the registration just one working day before candidate lists for the 2013 Chamber of Deputies elections were due, and the DGPR was unable to register candidates for the election. DGPR leaders reported the party was permitted to publish policy proposals as alternatives to RPF policy and hold small meetings with party supporters. Local officials, however, often threatened DGPR members with dismissal from employment or the withholding of state services unless they left the party. In 2014 the organizing secretary for DGPR, Jean Damascene Munyeshyaka, disappeared after meeting with an unknown individual in the town of Nyamata, Bugesera District. Police reported no developments regarding his disappearance during the year.

Party leaders for the unregistered opposition party Democratic Pact of the Imanzi People (PDP-Imanzi) and a splinter party, the People's Democratic Alliance (PDA), continued to seek permission to hold a founding party congress following the cancellation of the PDP-Imanzi congress in Gasabo District in 2013. The Ministry of Local Government and local officials continued to deny PDP-Imanzi and PDA permission to hold such a meeting, citing the two parties' connections to Deo Mushayidi, who remained incarcerated on state security charges (see section 1.e., Political Prisoners and Detainees).

The government no longer required but strongly encouraged all registered political parties to join the National Consultative Forum for Political Organizations, which sought to promote consensus among political parties, and required member parties to support publicly policy positions developed through dialogue. At year's end all registered parties were members of the organization. Government officials praised it for promoting political unity, while critics argued it stifled political competition and public debate.

Opposition leaders reported police arbitrarily arrested and beat some members of the unregistered Social Party-Imberakuri (Bernard Ntaganda faction), PDP-Imanzi, and FDU-Inkingi parties. Party members reported receiving threats because of their association with those parties.

In accordance with the constitution, which states a majority party in the Chamber of Deputies may not fill more than 50 percent of cabinet positions, independents and members of other political parties allied with the RPF held key positions in government, including that of prime minister and foreign minister. The Social Party-Imberakuri and the DGPR were not represented in the cabinet.

Participation of Women and Minorities: To register as a political party, an organization must present a list of at least 200 members, with at least five members in each of the 30 districts, and it must reserve at least 30 percent of its leadership positions for women.

Women secured 64 percent of seats in the 2013 Chamber of Deputies elections. Domestic observers noted, however, that lawmakers (male and female) in parliament's lower house appeared to lack capacity and power to influence policy or advance legislation.

Section 4. Corruption and Lack of Transparency in Government

The law provides criminal penalties for corruption by officials and private persons transacting business with the government that include imprisonment and fines. The law also allows citizens who report requests for bribes by government officials to receive financial rewards when officials are prosecuted; however, there were no reported cases of such rewards being given. While the government implemented anticorruption laws and encourage citizens to report requests for bribes, corruption remained a problem.

<u>Corruption</u>: Transparency International Rwanda and other NGOs reported the government investigated and prosecuted reports of corruption among police and government officials. Police frequently conducted internal investigations of police corruption, including sting operations, and punished offenders. The Office of the Ombudsman reported the government obtained 987 convictions for corruption-related offenses from 2011 to 2016, including 61 individuals who were convicted in the first quarter of 2016. The NPPA processed 200 corruption cases in 2015-16, with charges filed in 121 of them. Journalists and other observers noted corruption investigations focused exclusively on local officials and private persons; the government did not prosecute any senior officials for corruption during the year.

Embezzlement is a criminal offense that is litigated separately from other corruption-related crimes. The NPPA reported 483 convictions stemming from 258 cases of embezzlement in 2015-16. A total of 128 individuals were either acquitted of embezzlement or had charges dropped due to insufficient evidence during the year.

In July police arrested the former mayor of Gicumbi District on suspicion of embezzlement. During the year the NPPA and the Office of the Ombudsman opened investigations into 110 local leaders and government officials for corruption and embezzlement of up to 500 million Rwandan francs ($617,000) from government programs to aid the poor. There were reports district officials manipulated health insurance enrollment and socioeconomic classification statistics to appear to meet development targets, and observers noted some of the funds likely went missing due to mismanagement rather than theft.

International and domestic investors reported the government strongly supported the establishment of businesses, including through one-stop business licensing efforts that generally resulted in business registration within 72 hours. Nevertheless, investors reported contract disputes with the government and arbitrary enforcement of tax, immigration, and investment rules.

The NPPA prosecuted civil servants, police, and other officials for fraud, petty corruption, awarding of public tenders illegally, and mismanagement of public assets. Under the Ministry of Justice, the NPPA is also responsible for prosecuting police abuse cases. The RNP Inspectorate of Services investigated cases of police misconduct, and in 2014 the RNP launched an anticorruption unit. Authorities arrested two police officers on corruption charges during the year and dismissed another 33 in December 2015 for misconduct, indiscipline, and abuse of power. In August the government also dismissed with disgrace 14 RCS officers for gross misconduct and corruption. The RNP advertised a toll-free hotline number on local radio and in the press and provided deposit boxes in many communities to encourage citizens to report both positive and negative police and DASSO behavior.

The Office of the Auditor General worked to prevent corruption, including by investigating improper ministerial tendering practices. The RNP and the NPPA used the auditor general's annual report to pursue investigations into government-owned businesses. The Office of the Ombudsman led the National Anticorruption Council and had an active good governance program and several local-level anticorruption units. In 2013 the Office of the Ombudsman was granted legal authority to prosecute corruption cases but had prosecuted only one case. The Rwanda Governance Board monitored governance more broadly and promoted mechanisms to control corruption. The Rwanda Revenue Authority's Anticorruption Unit had a code of conduct and an active mechanism for internal discipline. The National Tender Board, Rwanda Utilities Regulatory Authority, and National Bureau of Standards also enforced their own regulations.

The government utilized a "bagging and tagging" system to aid companies with regional and international due diligence requirements related to conflict minerals. The government maintained a ban on the purchase or sale of undocumented minerals from neighboring countries. Observers and government officials reported smugglers trafficked an unknown amount of undocumented minerals through the country.

Financial Disclosure: The constitution and law require annual reporting of income and assets by public officials as well as reporting them upon entering and leaving office. There is no requirement for public disclosure of those assets, except in cases where irregularities are discovered. The Office of the Ombudsman, which monitors and verifies disclosures, reported 99 percent of officials complied with the requirement in 2015. In cases of noncompliance, the Office of the Ombudsman has the power to garnish wages and impose administrative sanctions that often involved loss of position or prosecution.

Public Access to Information: The government promulgated the Access to Information Law in 2013. The law grants wide access to government information upon request and in some cases to information held by private entities when disclosure is deemed to be in the public interest. The government may limit access to information if its release is considered to be against the public interest or if the information pertains to national security, as determined by the Prosecutor

General's Office. As of October the access to information portal *Sobanukirwa*, which was launched in 2015, indicated that of 108 requests for information submitted to the government, 14 received replies.

Section 5. Governmental Attitude Regarding International and Nongovernmental Investigation of Alleged Violations of Human Rights

Several domestic and international human rights groups operated in the country, investigating and publishing their findings on human rights cases. The government was often intolerant of public reports of human rights violations and suspicious of local and international human rights observers, and it often impeded independent investigations and rejected criticism as biased and uninformed. Human rights NGOs expressed fear of the government, reported SSF monitoring of their activities, and self-censored their comments. NGOs working on human rights and deemed to be critical of the government experienced difficulties securing or renewing required legal registration.

The government criticized HRW, Reporters Without Borders, the Committee to Protect Journalists, the Institute for War and Peace Reporting, Freedom House, and Amnesty International for being inaccurate and biased. Following the 2015 publication of HRW's report on the Gikondo Transit Center, the government revoked its Memorandum of Understanding (MOU) with HRW and suspended HRW's registration, forcing the HRW head researcher to leave the country and fire HRW's local staff. In June the government signed a new MOU with HRW; however, it did not act on HRW's application for renewed registration. After an initial four-week trip in April and May to conclude and sign the MOU, HRW's head researcher was unable to obtain a visa to re-enter the country for either work or tourism purposes. HRW had not renewed operations by year's end.

The government conducted surveillance on some international and domestic NGOs. Some NGOs reported authorities pressured individuals affiliated with them to provide information on their activities and expressed concern that intelligence agents infiltrated their organizations to gather information, influence leadership decisions, or create internal problems.

Several domestic NGOs that contributed reports to the country's *Second Universal Periodic Review on Human Rights* (UPR) in 2015 reported the SSF temporarily detained and questioned members of the groups on content deemed to be critical of the government's human rights record. Some individuals reported being threatened with arrest and prosecution for the contents of their reports. Due to SSF intimidation and harassment, several organizations disavowed their contributions to the review during the year, publicly retracting their criticism of the government's human rights record.

A few domestic NGOs--including the League for the Protection of Human Rights, Youth Association for Human Rights Promotion and Development, Rwandan Association for the Defense of Human Rights, and League for Human Rights in the Great Lakes Region (LDGL)--nominally focused on human rights abuses, but their effectiveness was limited due to internal conflict and self-censorship.

On May 28, Epimack Kwokwo, a Congolese national and the LDGL's former executive secretary, was expelled after the government refused his work visa application, which was submitted in October 2015. The LDGL was unable to carry out any programming between February, when its registration lapsed, and November when it was renewed, and the organization succumbed to controversy, with many members alleging the government manipulated the board elections to insert progovernment members into the leadership.

A progovernment NGO, the Rwanda Civil Society Platform, managed and directed some NGOs through umbrella groups that theoretically aggregated NGOs working in particular thematic sectors. Many observers believed the government controlled some of the umbrella groups.

In 2014 the Office of the Prime Minister published regulations that required NGOs to participate in joint action and development forums at the district and sector level. The regulations granted local government broad powers to regulate activities, levy fees, and bar organizations that did not comply. NGO leaders expressed concern the forums' structure might further tighten government control over NGO activities; the government responded the structure was intended to coordinate but not direct their activities.

In 2012 the government passed two NGO laws. The law on local NGOs moved their oversight from the Ministry of Local Government to the Rwanda Governance Board, replaced annual registration with one-time registration, and required submission of annual budgets and reports. The law on international NGOs allows for registration in up to five-year increments, depending on the duration of an NGO's funding, but provides for oversight by the Directorate General of Immigration and Emigration. The government granted only single-year registration to many international NGOs, including most involved in human rights, democratic institution building, and other advocacy issues. It also limited the

number of visas issued to the foreign staff of some international NGOs.
International NGOs in the health, education, and development sectors did not face
similar impediments.

Local and international NGOs often experienced difficulties obtaining registration,
in part because the process required submission of a statement of objectives, plan
of action, and detailed financial information for each district in which an NGO
wished to operate. International NGOs reported the government used the
registration process to delay programming and pressure them into financially
supporting government programs and policies. The regulatory environment
worsened during the year for international NGOs focused on advocacy, the
promotion of media freedom and human rights, and expansion of civic
engagement. Some international NGOs were obliged to cancel their programming
after experiencing registration delays of a year or more.

The United Nations or Other International Bodies: The government sometimes
cooperated with international human rights bodies but criticized the UN Group of
Experts on the DRC, claiming it was inaccurate and biased.

Government Human Rights Bodies: The independent and adequately funded
Office of the Ombudsman operated with the cooperation of executive agencies and
took action on cases of corruption and other abuses, including human rights cases
(see section 4).

The government funded and cooperated with the NHRC. According to many
observers, the NHRC did not have adequate resources to investigate all reported
violations and remained biased in favor of the government. Some victims of
human rights abuses did not report abuses to the NHRC because they perceived it
as biased and feared retribution by the SSF.

In 2012 the International Criminal Tribunal for Rwanda, based in Tanzania,
transferred its remaining genocide cases to a Tanzania-based branch of the
Mechanism for International Criminal Tribunals that continued to pursue genocide
suspects. From 1994 through year's end, the tribunal completed 75 cases; of these,
52 were convictions, 11 were convictions pending appeal, and 12 were acquittals.
Eight suspects remained fugitives.

Section 6. Discrimination, Societal Abuses, and Trafficking in Persons

Women

<u>Rape and Domestic Violence</u>: The law criminalizes rape and spousal rape, and the government handled rape cases as a judicial priority. Penalties for conviction of rape range from five years' to life imprisonment with fines of 500,000 to one million Rwandan francs ($617 to $1,234). Penalties for spousal rape range from two months to life imprisonment with fines of 100,000 to 300,000 Rwandan francs ($123 to $370).

The law provides for imprisonment of three to six months for threatening, harassing, or beating one's spouse. Domestic violence against women was common. Authorities encouraged the reporting of domestic violence cases, although most incidents remained within the extended family and were not reported or prosecuted. The NPPA reported 190 cases of rape; 182 of these were prosecuted during the year, resulting in 152 convictions. The NPPA also reported 448 cases of spousal abuse that resulted in 338 prosecutions; of these, 319 cases resulted in convictions; the remaining 19 were dismissed for lack of evidence.

Police headquarters in Kigali had a hotline for domestic violence. Several other ministries also had free GBV hotlines. Each of the 78 police stations nationwide had its own gender desk, an average of three officers trained in handling domestic violence and GBV cases, and a public outreach program. The RNP Directorate against GBV handled all cases of such violence and child protection. The government established 29 one-stop centers throughout the country, providing medical, psychological, legal, and police assistance at no cost to victims of domestic violence. The government expanded the network of one-stop centers in hospitals, districts, and refugee camps.

The government conducted a whole-of-government, multistakeholder campaign against GBV, child abuse, and other types of domestic violence. GBV was a required training module for police and military at all levels and was included as a module for all troops and police deploying to peacekeeping missions abroad.

<u>Female Genital Mutilation/Cutting (FGM/C)</u>: According to the UN Office for the Coordination of Humanitarian Affairs, FGM/C was not traditionally practiced in the country. The government ratified the Maputo Protocol to the African Charter on Human and Peoples' Rights on the Rights of Women in Africa (2003), which prohibits "all forms of female genital mutilation, scarification, medicalization and paramedicalization of female genital mutilation, and all other practices in order to eradicate them."

The law considers all sex-based practices carried out on children, regardless of form or method and including FGM/C, to be defilement punishable if convicted by life in prison and a fine of 100,000 to one million Rwandan francs ($123 to $1,234). There were no reports of FGM/C perpetrated against children during the year.

Sexual Harassment: The law prohibits sexual harassment by employers or any other person and provides for penalties for conviction of two months' to two years' imprisonment and fines from 100,000 to 500,000 Rwandan francs ($123 to $617). Nevertheless, advocacy organizations reported sexual harassment remained common. The City of Kigali conducted a program to combat sexual harassment of women and girls in public spaces, and government officials frequently spoke publicly against sexual harassment and GBV.

Reproductive Rights: The government encouraged couples to have no more children than they could afford but also respected the right of couples and individuals to decide freely and responsibly the number, spacing, and timing of children; manage their reproductive health; and have the information and means to do so, free from discrimination, coercion, and violence.

According to the United Nations, the estimated maternal mortality ratio decreased from 340 deaths per 100,000 live births in 2010 to 290 in 2015, with a lifetime risk of maternal death of one in 66. Major factors influencing maternal mortality included lack of access to health facilities due to cost or distance, and unhygienic conditions.

The UN Population Division estimated 46.7 percent of girls and women ages 15-49 used a modern method of contraception in 2015.

The NGO Ipas and the Great Lakes Initiative for Human Rights Development reported in 2015 that an average of 25 percent of women in prison were serving sentences for illegal abortion and were often arrested after seeking emergency health care for the management of complications arising from abortion. The RCS disputed the findings, stating only 2 percent of women in prison were serving sentences for illegal abortion. In December the president pardoned 62 women and girls serving sentences for abortion; media reported they were under age 16 at the time of conviction.

Discrimination: Women have the same legal status and are entitled to the same rights as men, including under family, labor, nationality, and inheritance laws. The law allows women to inherit property from their fathers and husbands, and couples may make their own legal property arrangements. Women experienced some difficulties pursuing property claims due to lack of knowledge, procedural bias against women in inheritance matters, multiple spousal claims due to polygyny, and the threat of GBV. The law requires equal pay for equal work and prohibits discrimination in hiring decisions.

After the 1994 genocide, which left many women as heads of households, women assumed a larger role in the formal sector, and many operated their own businesses. According to the National Institute of Statistics' *2015 Integrated Household Living Conditions Survey*, women headed 26 percent of households, and 24 percent of these households were in the lowest socioeconomic category. Women's work was more concentrated in the agricultural sector, with 79 percent of women engaged in agricultural work, compared with 59 percent of men. Women worked in sales and commerce in similar proportion to men.

Women comprised 64 percent of the Chamber of Deputies and one-third of cabinet ministers but were a minority in district- and sector-level government positions. The 2015 organic law on cell- and sector-level mediation committees decreed that at least 30 percent of mediation committee members must be women. Men owned the major assets of most households, particularly those at the lower end of the economic spectrum, making bank credit inaccessible to many women and rendering it difficult to start or expand a business.

The government-funded National Women's Council served as a forum for women's issues and consulted with the government on land, inheritance, and child protection laws. The Ministry of Gender and Family Promotion led government programs to address women's issues and coordinated programs with other ministries, police, and NGOs, including the national action plan for the implementation of UN Security Council Resolution 1325 on women, peace, and security. The government provided scholarships for girls in primary and secondary school and loans to rural women. A number of women's groups actively promoted women and children's concerns, particularly those of widows, orphaned girls, and households headed by children. The government-run Gender Monitoring Office tracked the mainstreaming of gender equality and women's empowerment throughout all sectors of society and collected gender-disaggregated data to inform policy processes.

Children

<u>Birth Registration</u>: Children derive citizenship from their parents. Children born to two Rwandan parents automatically receive citizenship. Children with one Rwandan parent must apply for citizenship before turning 18. Children born in the country to unknown or stateless parents automatically receive citizenship. Minor children adopted by Rwandans, irrespective of nationality or statelessness, automatically receive citizenship. Children retain their citizenship in the event of dissolution of the parents' marriage. Births were registered at the sector level upon presentation of a medical birth certificate. There were no reports of unregistered births leading to denial of public services.

<u>Education</u>: The government implemented a 12-year basic education program in 2012 that extended free universal public education to six years of primary and six years of secondary education. Education through grade nine is compulsory. Parents were not required to pay tuition fees, although the LDGL reported in 2015 that "in practice parents have to pay high education fees for teachers' incentives and meal expenses." Radio programs echoed similar concerns throughout the year.

According to the *2015 Integrated Household Living Conditions Survey*, 88 percent of children attended primary school in 2013/14, and 23 percent attended secondary school. Attendance was higher among girls than boys for both levels of education: 89 percent for girls compared with 87 percent for boys in primary school, and 25 percent for girls compared with 21 percent for boys in secondary school.

<u>Child Abuse</u>: While statistics on child abuse were unreliable, such abuse was common within the family, in the village, and at school. The government conducted a high-profile public awareness campaign against GBV and child abuse. The government supported a network of one-stop centers and hospital facilities that offered integrated police, legal, medical, and counseling services to victims of GBV and child abuse.

The government reported all cases of child abuse under the broad heading of "defilement" regardless of whether the abuse was sexual in nature. From July 1, 2015, to June 30, the NPPA reported prosecuting 1,479 defilement cases; of these, 1,203 resulted in convictions and 276 in acquittals.

In May the NHRC released a report on sexual harassment and defilement of minors with the goal of establishing evidence-based mitigation strategies to combat GBV. Based on interviews with more than 200 child victims of sexual abuse and harassment, the report identified teachers and caretakers as the most common perpetrators of GBV while noting the study revealed extensive underreporting due to cultural reasons and fear of stigma.

Early and Forced Marriage: The minimum age for marriage is 21. Anecdotal evidence suggested child marriage was more common in rural areas and refugee camps than in urban areas.

Female Genital Mutilation/Cutting (FGM/C): For information for girls under 18, see Women's section above.

Sexual Exploitation of Children: The law states sexual relations with a child under age 18 constitute child defilement and are punishable if convicted by life in prison and a fine of 100,000 to one million Rwandan francs ($123 to $1,234). Between July 2015 and July 2016, the NPPA received 2,272 defilement cases; of these, 1,479 were prosecuted to conclusion, 437 cases were dismissed due to lack of evidence, and 356 remained in litigation at year's end.

The law prohibits commercial sexual exploitation of children and child pornography, which are punishable by penalties if convicted of six months to seven years' imprisonment and a fine of 500,000 to 20 million Rwandan francs ($617 to $24,700). Conviction statistics were not available. The government, however, reported prosecuting 30 human trafficking cases during the year, resulting in seven convictions and seven acquittals, with 16 cases undecided at year's end. Local media reports indicated victims in a number of these cases were minors.

Child Soldiers: There were no reports of RDF recruitment of Rwandan children as child soldiers. In contrast with the previous year, there were no confirmed reports of refugee children of Burundian origin recruited into armed groups.

The government supported the Musanze Child Rehabilitation Center in Northern Province that provided care and social reintegration preparation for children who previously served in armed groups in the DRC (see section 2.d., Emigration and Repatriation). The center provided education, psychosocial support, recreational and cultural activities, medical care, and agricultural vocational training.

Displaced Children: There were numerous street children throughout the country. Authorities gathered street children in district transit centers and placed them in rehabilitation centers. Conditions and practices varied at 29 privately run rehabilitation centers for street children.

UNHCR reported that approximately 1,500 unaccompanied children entered the country as part of an influx of more than 81,000 refugees from Burundi in 2015-16. UNHCR accommodated unaccompanied minors in the Mahama refugee camp and had camp staff provide them additional protection measures.

Institutionalized Children: The UN Children's Fund reported in 2014 that one privately run and 30 government-run childcare institutions provided shelter, basic needs, and rehabilitation for approximately 3,000 orphans and street children. According to the National Commission for Children, 70 percent of children in orphanages were not orphans but had either run away from or been abandoned by their families. The government worked with international organizations and NGOs to provide vocational training and psychosocial support to orphans and street children, reintegrate them into their communities, and educate parents on how to prevent their children from becoming street children.

International Child Abductions: The country is not a party to the 1980 Hague Convention on the Civil Aspects of International Child Abduction. See the Department of State's *Annual Report on International Parental Child Abduction* at travel.state.gov/content/childabduction/en/legal/compliance.html.

Anti-Semitism

There was a very small Jewish community, consisting entirely of foreigners, and there were no reports of anti-Semitic acts.

Trafficking in Persons

See the Department of State's *Trafficking in Persons Report* at www.state.gov/j/tip/rls/tiprpt/.

Persons with Disabilities

The law prohibits discrimination against persons with physical, sensory, intellectual, and mental disabilities in employment, education, air travel and other transportation, access to health care, the judicial system, and the provision of other state services, and the government generally enforced these provisions. The law also mandates access to public facilities, accommodations for taking national examinations, provision of medical care by the government, and monitoring of implementation by the NHRC. The government generally implemented all of the foregoing provisions. Despite a continuing campaign to create a barrier-free environment for persons with disabilities, accessibility remained a problem throughout the country, including in public buildings. For example, civil society groups reported a need for interpreters fluent in sign language in police stations and courts.

Many children with disabilities did not attend primary or secondary school. The National Council of Persons with Disabilities estimated in 2014 there were 3,500 primary school students in special centers established to serve children with disabilities. Few students with disabilities reached the university level because many primary and secondary schools were unable to accommodate their disabilities. Institutes of higher education admitted some students with disabilities, but only the National University of Rwanda and the Kigali Institute of Education were able to accommodate students with visual disabilities.

There was one government psychiatric referral hospital in Kigali, with district hospitals providing limited psychiatric services. All other mental health facilities were nongovernmental. Facilities were often underequipped and understaffed, although the government worked to improve staffing and equipment in health facilities throughout the country.

Some citizens viewed disability as a curse or punishment that could result in social exclusion and sometimes abandoned or hid children with disabilities from the community.

The National Council of Persons with Disabilities, which assisted government efforts to provide for the rights of persons with disabilities, designated one member with disabilities to the Chamber of Deputies. The National Union of Disability Organizations in Rwanda provided an umbrella civil society platform for advocacy on behalf of persons with disabilities. A disabilities coordination forum was organized every trimester.

Persons with mental disabilities were required to submit a medical certificate to be eligible to vote. Some disabilities advocates complained requirements for electoral candidates to hold secondary education diplomas or higher degrees, depending on position, disadvantaged persons with disabilities. Advocates for persons with disabilities raised concerns regarding exclusion of persons with disabilities from polling centers and denial of their applications to the NHRC to serve as election monitors.

National/Racial/Ethnic Minorities

Longstanding tensions in the country culminated in the 1994 state-orchestrated genocide that killed between 750,000 and one million citizens, including approximately three-quarters of the Tutsi population. Following the killing of the president in 1994, an extremist interim government directed the Hutu-dominated national army, militia groups, and ordinary citizens to kill resident Tutsis and moderate Hutus. The genocide ended later in 1994 when the predominantly Tutsi RPF, operating from Uganda and northern Rwanda, defeated the national army and Hutu militias and established an RPF-led government of national unity that included members of eight political parties.

Since 1994 the government has called for national reconciliation and abolished the policies of the former government that created and deepened ethnic cleavages. The government removed all references to ethnicity in official discourse--with the exception of references to the genocide, which is officially termed "the 1994 genocide against the Tutsi"--and eliminated ethnic quotas for education, training, and government employment.

Some individuals stated the government's reconciliation policies and programs failed to recognize Hutu victims of the genocide or stated crimes committed by the RPF after the end of the genocide.

The constitution provides for the eradication of ethnic, regional, and other divisions in society and the promotion of national unity. Most citizens know the regional or ethnic origin of their fellow citizens, and anecdotal reports suggested ethnic background played an important role in marriage, particularly in rural communities.

Indigenous People

Beginning in the 1920s, colonial authorities formally assigned "racial" categories to all citizens and required them to carry identity cards indicating their designated ethnicity: Hutu, Tutsi, or Twa. Government authorities continued this practice until after the 1994 genocide. The postgenocide government banned identity card references to ethnicity and prohibited social or political organizations based on ethnic affiliation. As a result the Twa, who number approximately 34,000, lost their official designation as an ethnic group. The government no longer recognizes groups advocating specifically for Twa needs, and some Twa believed this government policy denied them their rights as an indigenous ethnic group. Nonetheless, the government recognized the Community of Rwandan Potters, a registered NGO focused primarily on Twa community needs, as an advocate for the most marginalized. Most Twa lived on the margins of society with very limited access to health care and education.

Acts of Violence, Discrimination, and Other Abuses Based on Sexual Orientation and Gender Identity

There are no laws that criminalize sexual orientation or consensual same-sex sexual conduct, and cabinet-level government officials expressed support for the rights of lesbian, gay, bisexual, transgender, and intersex (LGBTI) persons. LGBTI persons reported societal discrimination and abuse, and LGBTI rights groups reported occasional harassment by neighbors and police.

There were no known reports of physical attacks against LGBTI persons, nor were there any reports of LGBTI persons fleeing the country due to harassment or attack.

HIV and AIDS Social Stigma

The constitution is silent on HIV-positive status; however, the penal code provides for imprisonment of up to six months for persons convicted of stigmatizing an individual who suffers from an incurable infection. There were no reports of prosecutions under this statute. Discrimination against persons with HIV/AIDS occurred, although such incidents remained rare. The government actively supported relevant public education campaigns, including establishing HIV/AIDS awareness clubs in secondary schools and making public pronouncements against stigmatization of those with the disease.

The penal code also provides stiffer penalties for conviction of rape and defilement in cases of transmission of an incurable illness. In most cases of sexual violence, the victim and alleged perpetrator both undergo HIV testing. The law provides penalties for conviction of 10 to 15 years' imprisonment in cases where an adult rape victim contracted an incurable disease; in cases where no transmission occurs, the penalty is typically five years' imprisonment. Conviction of rape with intention to infect another person with an incurable illness carries a 20- to 25-year prison sentence. The law provides for life imprisonment in cases where child defilement led to the transmission of an incurable disease.

According to RDF policy and in keeping with UN guidelines, the military did not permit its members with HIV/AIDS to participate in peacekeeping missions abroad but allowed them to remain in the RDF.

Section 7. Worker Rights

a. Freedom of Association and the Right to Collective Bargaining

The law provides that "every worker in every enterprise," except for certain senior public servants, police, and soldiers, has the right to form and join independent unions, conduct legal strikes, and bargain collectively. The law also permits informal-sector workers to join unions, conduct strikes, and bargain collectively, but informal workers are exempt from other protections of the law. Most provisions of the law generally do not protect unregistered small business, cooperatives, and informal-sector workers.

The law restricts voluntary collective bargaining by requiring prior authorization or approval by authorities and requiring binding arbitration in cases of nonconciliation. The law allows unions to negotiate with employers for an industry-level minimum wage in certain sectors, but these agreements were not enforced.

The law provides some workers the right to conduct strikes, subject to numerous restrictions. Public servants, soldiers, and employees providing "essential services" generally are not permitted to strike, and participation in unauthorized demonstrations may result in employee dismissal, nonpayment of wages, and civil action against the union. A union's executive committee must approve any strike, and the union must first try to resolve its differences with management through complex compulsory arbitration, conciliation, and mediation processes prescribed by the Ministry of Public Service and Labor.

Other provisions of the law frequently abrogated these rights. For example, a ministerial order that broadly defines essential services to include public transportation, security, education (during national exams), water and sanitation, and telecommunications severely restricts the right to strike in these fields.

Ministerial orders define the implementation of the labor law; there are no significant inconsistencies between the law and ministerial orders. All unions must register with the Ministry of Public Service and Labor. The application process was cumbersome, lengthy, and costly, and it required unions to disclose their membership and property.

The law allows unions to conduct activities without interference, prohibits antiunion discrimination, and requires employers to reinstate workers fired for union activity. Conviction of antiunion interference and discrimination are subject to penalties of up to two months in prison and fines of 50,000 to 300,000 Rwandan francs ($62 to $370), which were not sufficient to deter violations.

There were 29 labor unions organized into three confederations: 15 unions were represented by the Rwanda Confederation of Trade Unions (CESTRAR), seven by the Labor and Worker's Brotherhood Congress (COTRAF), and seven by the National Council of Free Trade Union Organizations in Rwanda. All three federations ostensibly were independent, but CESTRAR had close links to the government and the ruling RPF party.

Freedom of association and the right to collective bargaining generally were not respected. The government did not enforce applicable laws effectively and restricted these rights.

The government severely limited the right to collective bargaining, and legal mechanisms were inadequate to protect this right. Labor union officials commented that many private-sector businesses controlled by the RPF or the RDF were off limits to collective bargaining negotiations. The government also controlled collective bargaining with cooperatives. No labor union had an established collective bargaining agreement with the government.

Collective bargaining occasionally was practiced in the private sector. For example, in 2015 an international tea exporter renewed its 2012 collective bargaining agreement with its employees. CESTRAR, COTRAF, and the Ministry of Public Service and Labor participated in the negotiations.

There were neither registered strikes nor anecdotal reports of unlawful strikes during the year; the last recorded strike was by textile workers in 2013.

National elections for trade union representatives were held in 2015. Trade union leaders stated the government interfered in the elections and pressured some candidates not to run.

There were no functioning labor courts or other formal mechanisms to resolve antiunion discrimination complaints, and COTRAF reported it could take four to five years for labor disputes to be resolved through the civil courts. According to several trade unions, employers in small companies frequently used transfers, demotions, and dismissals to intimidate union members.

b. Prohibition of Forced or Compulsory Labor

The law prohibits most forms of forced or compulsory labor, and the government generally enforced the law. In 2014 the government issued a national trafficking in persons action plan that included programs to address forced labor. The penal code criminalizes human trafficking under a variety of articles. The law prescribes penalties for conviction of seven to 10 years' imprisonment or fines ranging from 5,444,600 to 10,958,120 Rwandan francs ($6,722 to $13,528) for internal trafficking, and up to 15 years' imprisonment for transnational trafficking. Penalties are sufficiently stringent and commensurate with those prescribed for other serious crimes. Child trafficking convictions are subject to a minimum five-year prison term, while slavery convictions carry three- to 12-year prison terms. Statistics on the number of victims removed from forced labor were not available.

Also see the Department of State's annual *Trafficking in Persons Report* at www.state.gov/j/tip/rls/tiprpt/.

c. Prohibition of Child Labor and Minimum Age for Employment

The minimum age for full-time employment is 16. The law prohibits children under age 18 from participating in hazardous work, defined as night work from 7 p.m. to 5 a.m.; the worst forms of child labor as defined under International Labor Organization Convention 182; or any work deemed difficult, unsanitary, or dangerous by the Ministry of Public Service and Labor. Prohibited sectors include work in industrial institutions, domestic service, mining and quarrying, construction, brick making, or applying fertilizers and pesticides. The law prohibits forced or compulsory labor by children; children in military service, prostitution, or pornography; and child trafficking and slavery. The law provides for working children to have at least 12 hours of rest between work periods. The law provides six months to 20 years' imprisonment and fines of 500,000 to five million Rwandan francs ($617 to $6,173) for violations. The law applies to contractual employment but not to noncontractual employment, such as subsistence family farming or casual labor in agricultural cooperatives, and thus leaves most working children unprotected. In addition to national law, some districts enforced local regulations against hazardous child labor and sanctioned employers and parents for violations. The government did not enforce the law effectively. Police, immigration officials, local government officials, and labor inspectors received training on identifying victims of trafficking.

The National Commission for Children (NCC) took the lead role in designating responsible agencies and establishing actions to be taken, timelines, and other concrete measures in relation to the integrated child rights policy and various national commissions, plans, and policies related to child protection subsumed therein. At the local level, 149 child labor committees monitored incidents of child labor, and each district was required to establish a steering committee to combat child labor. At the village level, 320 child labor focal point volunteers were appointed, supported by 10 national protection officers appointed by the NCC and 48 social workers. A domestic NGO completed a survey on child labor under NCC supervision in July, but it had not made the results public by year's end. Similarly, a different NGO completed a targeted survey of the prevalence of child labor in tea-growing districts, but the survey results, presented to the Ministry of Public Service and Labor in March, remained unpublished at year's end. The ministry conducted labor inspections of firms previously known to employ children, focusing on companies operating in the mining, construction, and agriculture sectors. The RNP operated a Child Protection Unit. District government officials, as part of their performance contracts, enforced child labor reduction and school attendance benchmarks.

The government worked with NGOs to raise awareness of the problem and to identify and send to school or vocational training children involved in child labor. The Ministry of Public Service and Labor invited private-sector businesses to sign a memorandum of understanding committing them to eradicate child labor. The government's 12-year basic education program aided in reducing the incidence of child labor, although many children who worked also attended school because classes were held in alternating morning or afternoon shifts. The government fined those who illegally employed children or parents who sent their children to work instead of school. Teachers and local authorities received training on the rights of children and other human rights. The ministry raised public awareness of the worst forms of child labor through radio shows, television announcements, and skits. Government efforts to stop child prostitution included a high-profile public campaign to discourage intergenerational sex and sexual procurement.

The majority of child laborers worked in the agricultural sector and as household domestics. Child labor also existed in isolated instances in small companies and light manufacturing, in cross-border transportation, and in the brick making, charcoal, rock crushing, and mining industries. Children received low wages, and abuse was common. In addition trafficking of children, including child prostitution, were problems.

Also see the Department of Labor's *Findings on the Worst Forms of Child Labor* at www.dol.gov/ilab/reports/child-labor/findings/.

d. Discrimination with Respect to Employment and Occupation

The law prohibits discrimination based on race, ethnicity, national origin, gender, marital status, religion, political affiliation, pregnancy, disability, socioeconomic status, age, and "any other type of discrimination." The law does not specifically protect sexual orientation, gender identity, and HIV-positive status. The constitution requires equal pay for equal work.

The government sought to enforce antidiscrimination laws, but there were numerous reports not challenged in court of discrimination based on gender, pregnancy, disability, and political affiliation. Migrant workers enjoyed the same legal protections, wages, and working conditions as citizens.

e. Acceptable Conditions of Work

During the year the National Labor Council approved a proposal to increase the national minimum wage, which would be the first revision to the minimum wage since 1974, when it was set at 100 Rwandan francs ($0.12) per day. The government, however, did not publish the new minimum wage by October. The Ministry of Public Service and Labor set industry-specific minimum wages in the small formal sector. For example, the minimum wage in the tea industry ranged from 500 to 1,000 Rwandan francs ($0.61 to $1.23) per day, while in the construction industry it ranged from 1,500 to 5,000 Rwandan francs ($1.85 to $6.17) a day, depending on skill level. Sector minimum wages were not enforced. Minimum wages provided a higher standard of living than that of the approximately 80 percent of the population relying on subsistence farming. As the country's largest employer, the government effectively set most other formal-sector wage rates.

According to the *2015 Integrated Household Living Conditions Survey*, the percentage of citizens in 2014 living below the poverty line was 39 percent, and the percentage living in extreme poverty was 16 percent.

The law provides a standard workweek of 45 hours and 18 to 21 days paid annual leave, in addition to official holidays. The law provides for premium pay for overtime for some salaried employees and sets prohibitions on excessive compulsory overtime, but these provisions often were disregarded and rarely enforced. The law provides employers with the right to determine daily rest periods. Most employees received a one-hour lunch break.

During the year the labor law was amended to provide fully paid maternity leave for up to three months. In February the government required formal-sector employees to contribute 0.3 percent of their salary to a fund to support maternity benefits; employers are required to match employee contributions on a one-to-one basis.

The law regulates hours of work and occupational health and safety standards in the formal-wage sector. Ministerial orders determine the modalities for establishing and operating occupational safety and health committees, but the committees had not been established. The same labor standards applied to migrant and foreign workers as to citizens.

The ministry had 35 labor inspectors, with at least one in each district, who reported to district mayors. Inspectors did not enforce labor standards effectively. The many violations reported to labor unions compared to the few actions taken by the government and employers to remedy substandard working conditions suggested penalties were insufficient to deter violations.

Some workers accepted less than the minimum wage. Families regularly supplemented their incomes by working in small businesses or subsistence agriculture. Most workers in the formal sector worked six days per week. Violations of wage, overtime, and occupational health and safety standards were common in both the formal and informal sectors. Local media highlighted the common problem of employers not registering employees for social security or occupational health insurance and not paying into those benefit systems as required by law. Workers in the subcontractor and business process outsourcing sectors were especially vulnerable to hazardous or exploitative working conditions. Statistics on workplace fatalities and accidents were not available, but ministry officials singled out mining as a sector with significant problems in implementing occupational safety and health standards. There were no major industrial accidents during the year.

Workers did not have explicit rights to remove themselves from situations that endangered their health or safety without jeopardizing their jobs. The Ministry of Public Safety and Labor sought to promote the health and safety of workers by maintaining a list of dangerous professions subject to heightened safety scrutiny.